TRAUMA

Dan Hughes
with Matthew Blythe

ADOPTION & FOSTERING ACADEMY

Published by
CoramBAAF Adoption and Fostering Academy
41 Brunswick Square
London WC1N 1AZ
www.corambaaf.org.uk

Coram Academy Limited, registered as a company limited by
guarantee in England and Wales number 9697712, part of the
Coram group, charity number 312278

British Library Cataloguing in Publication Data
A catalogue record for this book is available from the British Library

ISBN 978 1 910039 50 2

Project management by Shaila Shah, Director of Publications,
CoramBAAF
Designed and typeset by Fravashi Aga
Printed in Great Britain by the Lavenham Press
Trade distribution by Turnaround Publisher Services, Unit 3,
Olympia Trading Estate, Coburg Road, London N22 6TZ

Contents

Looking behind the label…

SECTION I

UNDERSTANDING THE EFFECTS OF
CHILDHOOD TRAUMA   I

1 What constitutes trauma in childhood?   3

2 Symptoms, prognosis and treatment   5

3 Frequently asked questions   20

4 Specific parenting tasks   25

5 How the child might be affected
   at different stages of development   37

6 Educational and social issues   40

7 Conclusion   43

   References   48

SECTION II

PARENTING CHILDREN AFFECTED BY
CHILDHOOD TRAUMA   49

The early years   51

Primary years   57

Secondary years   66

Useful organisations   88

Notes about the authors

For most of his professional life, **Dr Dan Hughes** has been a clinician specialising in the treatment of children and young people with severe emotional and behavioural problems. His treatment is family-centred, with the parents actively involved in their child's treatment, as well as addressing their own attachment histories. Working primarily with fostered and adopted children and their carers and parents, Dan borrowed heavily from attachment, intersubjectivity, and trauma theories and research to develop a model of treatment that he calls Dyadic Developmental Psychotherapy (known as Attachment-Focused Family Therapy when used as a general model of family therapy). Dan is the author of a number of books and articles including: *Building the Bonds of Attachment* (2nd edn) (2006, Jason Aronson); *Attachment-Focused Parenting* (2009, WW Norton) and *Attachment-Focused Family Therapy Workbook* (2011, WW Norton). More recently, he has published a book of poetry, *It was that One Moment...* (2012, Worth Publishing), focusing on the children and families he has treated. In 2012, he wrote *Brain-Based Parenting* with Jon Baylin (WW Norton) and *Creating Loving Connections*, with Kim Golding (Jessica Kingsley Publishers). He has also authored another title in the Parenting Matters series, *Parenting a Child with Emotional and Behavioural Difficulties*, for BAAF in 2012.

Dan's current passion is the training of therapists in his treatment model. He has provided therapist training throughout the US, UK, Canada and other countries for the past 18 years. He also provides ongoing supervision and consultation to various clinicians and agencies. Dan has initiated a certification programme for therapists interested in becoming proficient in his model of treatment.
Dan's website is: **www.danielhughes.org**
For information on Dyadic Development Psychotherapy:
ddpnetwork.org

Matthew Blythe I work in health care, and have had many years of professional experience of looking after people from a wide range of backgrounds. Around 10 years ago I changed jobs and moved house. Having not been fortunate enough to have had children, I started to look into adoption. I knew of a couple of single people who had adopted and thought I would see if I could. The rest is history!

I live on the south coast. I still love walks by the sea – it helps me re-attune. I am a member of a very supportive group of single adopters. We help, support and listen to each other. If I could offer one piece of advice, it would be to look after yourself, then you will be able to look after those around you.

The series editor

Hedi Argent is an established author/editor for CoramBAAF (previously BAAF). Her books cover a wide range of family placement topics and she has written several guides and a story book for young children.

Looking behind the label…

Jack has mild learning difficulties and displays some characteristics of ADHD and it is uncertain whether this will increase…

Beth and Mary both have a diagnosis of global developmental delay…

Abigail's birth mother has a history of substance abuse. There is no clear evidence that Abigail was prenatally exposed to drugs but her new family will have to accept some kind of developmental uncertainty…

Jade has some literacy and numeracy difficulties, but has made some improvement with the support of a learning mentor…

Prospective adopters and carers are often faced with the prospect of having to decide whether they can care for a child with a health need or condition they know little about and have no direct experience of. No easy task…

Will Jack's learning difficulties become more severe?
Will Beth and Mary be able to catch up?
When will it be clear whether or not Abigail has been affected by parental substance misuse?
And will Jade need a learning mentor throughout her school life?

It can be difficult to know where to turn for reliable information. What lies behind the diagnoses and "labels" that many looked after children bring with them? And what will it be like to live with them? How will they benefit from family life?

Parenting Matters is a unique series, "inspired" by the terms used – and the need to "decode" them – in profiles of children needing new permanent families. Each title provides expert knowledge about a particular condition, coupled with facts, figures and guidance presented in a straightforward and accessible style. Each book also describes what it is like to parent an affected child, with adopters and foster carers "telling it like it is", sharing their parenting experiences, and offering useful advice. This combination of expert information and first-hand experiences will help readers to gain understanding, and to make informed decisions.

Titles in the series deal with a wide range of health conditions and steer readers to where they can find more information. They offer a sound introduction to the topic under consideration and offer a glimpse of what it would be like to live with a "labelled" child. Most importantly, this series looks behind the label and give families the confidence to look more closely at a child whom they otherwise might have passed by.

Keep up with new titles as they are published by signing up to our newsletter on www.corambaaf.org.uk/bookshop.

Shaila Shah

Titles in this series include:

- *Parenting a Child with Attention Deficit Hyperactivity Disorder*

- *Parenting a Child with Dyslexia*

- *Parenting a Child with Mental Health Issues*

- *Parenting a Child Affected by Parental Substance Misuse*

- *Parenting a Child with Emotional and Behavioural Difficulties*

- *Parenting a Child with Autism Spectrum Disorder*

- *Parenting a Child with Developmental Delay*

- *Parenting a Child with or at risk of a Genetic Disease*

- *Parenting a Child affected by Domestic Violence*

- *Parenting a Child affected by Sexual Abuse*

UNDERSTANDING THE EFFECTS OF CHILDHOOD TRAUMA

DAN HUGHES

CHAPTER 1

What constitutes trauma in childhood?

The definition of trauma

Your child is considered to have been traumatised when she has experienced an extremely stressful event or events that overwhelmed her mind and disrupted the normal functioning of her emotions, cognition, behaviour, and/or bodily systems. Along with this dysregulated functioning, she is likely to be hyper-vigilant, with intrusive memories, while at the same time seeming to be emotionally numb, cognitively confused, and very avoidant of many situations.

Simple trauma
The trauma is considered to be a simple trauma when it involves one event that disrupts a child's life that is usually characterised by safety. Examples would include being bitten by a dog, an accident, an intrusive medical procedure, and the loss of an important person in the child's life.

Complex trauma: developmental trauma

The trauma is considered to be a complex trauma when it involves more than one event, when it is likely to have been ongoing, and the events compromise the child's sense of safety for a period of time. More recently, some mental health professionals have proposed the term "developmental trauma" to refer to interpersonal, intra-familial trauma. Developmental trauma would refer most specifically to children who have experienced abuse and/or neglect in their relationships with their primary caregivers. This trauma tends to have the most serious consequences, and it is also the one most likely to affect children who have had to be removed from their homes and families.

CHAPTER 2

Symptoms, prognosis and treatment

Symptoms

There are general effects of trauma in children, many of which are also present in traumatised adults. These include:

- Intrusive thoughts and emotions, flashbacks, memories, nightmares, re-enactments of the trauma in play and behaviour

- Sleep disturbance

- Emotional numbing

- Hypervigilance and increased arousal

- Avoidance of situations, people or objects associated with traumatic events

- Altered cognitive functioning, including confusion,

inattentiveness, obsessions, forgetfulness

- Behavioural extremes of impulsivity and inhibitions

- Regression to a younger level of functioning

- Impairment of relationships and home/school functioning

According to the diagnostic manual for mental health professionals, a child is not considered to manifest symptoms of trauma unless they are present for more than a month. Also, one or more symptoms of intrusive thoughts, hypervigilance and emotional numbing must be present for the child's functioning to be considered to be due to a trauma.

Developmental trauma, a common result of child abuse and neglect, is considered to have more severe, pervasive and longer lasting effects than simple traumas. The effects of developmental trauma, called the domains of impairment, are the following (Cook et al, 2005):

Attachment disturbances

It is hard to imagine how a child who is experiencing abuse and neglect at the hands of their parents could develop a secure attachment relationship with those same caregivers. However, attachment behaviour is activated even when a child is being traumatised, and initially the child turns to their caregiver, who also happens to be their abuser, for comfort and safety. After a time, this attachment behaviour becomes very unstable, leading to the disorganisation of the attachment pattern. However, attachment disorganisation is a classification given to the majority of young children entering foster care after experiencing abuse and neglect. This classification is considered to be a risk factor for the development of mental health problems in adolescence and adulthood. These problems involve both externalisation behaviours

(ADHD, oppositional-defiant disorder, conduct disorder, and explosive outbursts) as well as internalisation behaviours (disorders of depression, anxiety and dissociation).

Biology

The child being traumatised in his own home is likely to manifest problems with basic physiological regulation (bowel and urinary, appetite and sleep) as well as having extreme reactions to physical pain – both terror and/or no sensation of pain. Some children confuse being full with being hungry. Others do not feel the pain of an ear infection or a leg bruise. Some who do feel a pain in a part of their body become angry and hit the part that is painful, making it worse!

Affect regulation

Through safety and a secure attachment to his caregivers, a child learns how to regulate his emotional states and their affective expression. Traumatised children often experience rage rather than anger, terror rather than fear, and despair rather than sadness. They have difficulty regulating positive emotions as well. Often excitement, joy or love cause them to experience significant anxiety. They often cannot tolerate very exciting holidays such as visiting Disney World, sometimes taking weeks or months afterwards to become stable again. This dysregulation is likely to be greatest for younger children or children who have not developed their affect regulation skills well for other reasons.

Dissociation

When a child is being abused by his own parent, his best option is to dissociate. Other defensive reactions to the threat – aggression or flight – are not likely to be effective in reducing pain. In dissociation a child is able to mentally turn away from the present reality and not experience the present pain. He is not conscious of the terror that he is experiencing or, even, his bodily pain. One girl who had been traumatised by her parents until the age

7

of seven did not feel the pain of an ear infection four years after the trauma stopped. The infection got worse and caused damage to her middle ear, requiring surgery. Her adoptive mother was reported for medical neglect for ignoring the girl's intense pain for two weeks. The mother did not ignore the pain, the girl herself did, and had never mentioned it to her mother or even felt it herself. Other children, upon reflecting on past events when they were being physically or sexually abused, could describe how they left their body and felt nothing, as from a distance, until the abuse stopped. Dissociation is a very adaptive strategy when a child is trapped in a situation of ongoing abuse and neglect.

When the child is safely in a foster or adoptive home, they often still dissociate under stress. Routine disappointments or discipline may lead to dissociation where the child seems to withdraw into daydreams. A child whose cat died may sit and stare for a long time but never cry. A child who is angry over discipline may react with out-of-control rage and truly will not remember anything that he said or did.

Behaviour control

Children who are being traumatised do not have the safety needed to focus on their own development. Children have to learn to regulate their emotional states, focus their attention, and develop goal-directed behavioural patterns that require inhibiting competing behaviours and delaying the pursuit of immediate pleasure for a more distant goal. Not having developed these neuro-behavioural skills, children are often very impulsive, showing behaviour that reacts, seemingly indiscriminately at times, to internal or external stimuli. Other abused children, having found that their impulsivity creates more abuse, habitually try to inhibit it. They seem to be frozen in anxious and rigid immobility or they are continuously trying to control their impulses through repetitive, compulsive behaviours.

Cognition

When a child experiences repetitive trauma at the hands of his caregivers, he focuses his attention almost exclusively on how to keep himself safe in a threatening environment. He is hypervigilant for any signs of danger, such as his caregivers' moods as well as whether they are angry with each other or about an event. He is likely to closely monitor his own behaviour so that he does not accidentally do something that might cause further abuse or neglect. As a result of this heightened awareness of his external environment regarding threats to his safety, he directs little attention to the external world with regard to learning about new things, having interesting or exciting experiences, or becoming spontaneously engaged in play and imagination. Finally, he also directs little awareness to his internal world of thoughts, feelings, wishes, plans, memories or judgements. His inner life is often lacking in its organisation, identification and the breadth and depth of interests and new learning. The ability to focus on his inner life is known as reflective functioning, and this important skill may be compromised.

At the same time, he is likely to be behind in developing his academic skills. He may have problems with reading or other specific learning disabilities. He may display problems with speech and language, auditory processing or sensory integration.

Self-concept

When a child is being traumatised by his parents, he will not be able to identify it as abuse. Rather, he will believe that he deserves the maltreatment, that he must have caused it even if he does not know how. He believes the belief of the perpetrator: that if he were not being bad, stupid or selfish, he would not have been hurt. Children abused by their parents are full of shame for who they are. Their self-concept is one in which they are evil, bad, unlovable and disgusting.

And the children who believe that they are bad are among
the healthier of the children being abused. Other children,
living from one unpredictable abusive event to the next, have a
difficult time developing a stable, continuous sense of self. Their
identity is too unstable to even have a sense of being bad. This
is most likely to be the case for children who have experienced
chronic neglect. Hour after hour, day after day, there is no one
who consistently interacts with them and responds to their
initiatives and expressions of their inner life of thought, emotions
and wishes. Healthy children develop a sense of self within the
reciprocal interactions with their parents. Without these daily,
ongoing interactions, the sense of self tends to be weak and in
pieces. Children who lack continuing initiatives and responses
from their parents lack a continuous sense of self. This is a central
reason why many abused and neglected children have such a hard
time with transitions. From place to place, activity to activity,
day to day, they almost seem to be starting over each time. As if
repeatedly asking: Who am I? How do I handle this? Do I like this?
Am I safe here?

Prognosis

Once the traumatic event(s) stops, the prognosis for the child to
return to their previous level of functioning ranges from good to
poor, depending on the severity of the trauma, the source of the
trauma, the degree of safety provided in the home environment
both prior to and following the traumatic event, and the availability
of appropriate treatment.

The prognosis for simple trauma will generally be more favourable,
with a shorter timeframe than the prognosis for complex or
developmental trauma. Being traumatised by a dog, on one
occasion, with capable and comforting parents who will ensure
that it does not happen again, is going to be much less damaging to

a child than being traumatised by his parents, again and again, while not having other parents to protect him.

Developmental trauma is certain to have a more difficult prognosis because the source of safety for the child is also the source of the trauma. The child has nowhere to turn. Also, the child has no reason to believe that the trauma will end, so he cannot begin the process of healing. Relying on himself, not on attachment figures, he develops ways to try to ensure his own safety. These become symptoms. Having developed them to try to ensure his own survival, he is likely to strongly resist giving them up, not trusting that new caregivers will provide for his safety.

If the child manifested psychological problems prior to the traumatic event(s), the prognosis is likely to be less favourable than if the child manifested healthy development prior to the event. If the child is not provided with a safe environment after the traumatic event, the prognosis is also likely to be less favourable than if the child does experience a safe environment after the event.

Treatment

Simple trauma

The treatment for simple trauma, with a child who functioned well prior to the trauma, is likely to be more narrowly focused on the trauma itself than is treatment for developmental trauma. The treatment for simple trauma will probably involve:

- a gradual, step-by-step exposure to the thoughts and emotions associated with the event, with the therapist assisting the child to remain regulated while recalling the event and its impact. This might also include exposure to the object or event itself (i.e. the child

11

bitten by a dog might be safely brought into proximity with another dog)

- developing competing strengths and coping strategies that will gradually replace the symptoms that have developed in reaction to the trauma

- consulting with the child's caregivers to ensure that they are providing the child with safety in his daily life.

The treatment of simple trauma often involves an approach that focuses on developing practical cognitive and behavioural strategies for the child to manage the effects of the trauma. Treatment might also include assisting the child to express the effects of the trauma in his play through metaphor. The treatment of simple trauma is enhanced if the child has a secure attachment to their primary caregivers.

For years, mental health professionals did not focus sufficiently on the possible presence of trauma in the development of children's psychological problems. Now, the consensus among mental health professionals is that the treatment of children with psychological problems needs to be trauma-informed, with trauma being present in either a primary or secondary degree in many instances.

Developmental trauma

The treatment of developmental trauma, secondary to abuse and neglect, is considered to be a more comprehensive treatment and likely to be of longer duration than the treatment of simple trauma.

Recommendations for best practice in the treatment of developmental trauma involve the following characteristics (Cook et al, 2005):

Safety

Since trauma represents the absence of safety, establishing a sense of safety is crucial before the child can successfully address the trauma. Failing to establish safety causes the risk of "re-traumatising" the child in the act of trying to help him.

Safety is best ensured interpersonally, with the therapist conveying sensitivity, warmth, empathy and compassion for the child. The predictability of the sessions regarding time, place and routines is important, as is the child having a sense of control over efforts to explore, address and resolve the traumatic experience. The wise therapist will also be a consultant to the child's caregivers and teachers regarding safety in the home and school. If the child feels safe with his caregiver, and if the caregiver has the emotional strength to provide comfort and support the child while the trauma is being explored in treatment, then preference should be given to having the caregiver present during some, if not all, of the sessions.

Self-regulation

Since developmental trauma often creates pervasive problems in the child's ability to regulate his emotions, as well as his cognition and behaviour, it is important to assist children in establishing their self-regulation abilities. Through research in developmental and neuropsychology, we know that children's self-regulation skills develop only after first having their affective states co-regulated by their safe caregivers. Therefore, it is likely to be the case that teaching these skills in therapy will not, at least initially, teach the child to self-regulate with cognitive and coping skills. Rather, the therapist, and the parent if present, will need to co-regulate the child's affective, cognitive and behavioural states in order to help him experientially learn to self-regulate.

Co-regulation requires that the therapist – and parent – remain regulated when they focus with the child on the past traumatic

13

events. They then match the child's affective experience (by having synchronised rhythmic vocal and facial expressions, along with breathing and moving to a similar rhythm). Through this synchronised matching, the child's affective state can become or remain regulated while distressing topics are being explored. After the child has had such co-regulation experiences, he is more likely to be able to utilise self-regulation exercises (such as breathing, visualisation, self-talk) when he is on his own.

Self-reflective information processing

The child who has experienced developmental trauma has had little opportunity to become aware of his inner life and therefore he often has great difficulty identifying, understanding or communicating to others what he thinks, feels or wants. One therapeutic goal is to deepen his reflective capacity and guide him towards self-insight and a greater ability to know and act on what is in his best interests.

Throughout the course of treatment, the therapist might frequently wonder aloud about the child's thoughts, feelings and wishes, and when the child is uncertain, will assist him to develop curiosity about who he is, along with what he thinks, feels and wants. The constant attitude of the therapist involves open curiosity about the child's inner life. The child should know that his inner life will not be evaluated but accepted as it is. This acceptance enables the child to safely explore thoughts that he has seldom allowed to surface or questioned. Through this open self-discovery, without worry about being judged, the child often begins to re-examine general assumptions about himself and develop greater self-awareness that is likely to result in greater self-understanding and self-acceptance. This enhanced self-awareness often leads the child to develop new wishes, dreams, plans and goals.

Traumatic experience integration

If the traumatic event is not integrated, the memory of it remains frozen in the brain – a psychological tumour – to be activated when something reminds the child of the trauma, but also at unpredictable times. Each time that memory is activated, the emotions and thoughts associated with it can be almost as strong as the original experience. The brain does not "forget" the trauma – it lies waiting to be aroused. In time, the thoughts and emotions associated with the trauma can become less overwhelming and have less impact on the child's daily life, but for this to happen, the trauma needs to be integrated into the overall meaning of his life.

When the traumatic experience is integrated, it becomes impacted by the many other non-traumatic experiences of the child's life. If a child was traumatised by his father, and that experience has become integrated into his life, then his new experiences with other caregivers, teachers, parents of friends, will all contradict his experience with his father. The child can trust that the other adults do not abuse him; why then did his father? It must mean that his father is different from the other adults. The child did not deserve the abuse; his father was wrong. If, however, the traumatic experience has not been integrated, then the meaning of the abuse – the child did deserve it, he can't trust other adults, his father was right – remains unchanged in spite of all the different experiences the child has. Foster carers and adopters are often discouraged when after months or even years of good care, their child still reacts with terror if he does something wrong, or rage because he thinks that they think that he is a bad boy. His view of himself and of them is still dominated by the experiences of abuse that remain alive and whole: a tumour in his brain.

How does the traumatic experience become integrated? Sometimes the contrast with safe experiences with other caregivers is sufficient. However, it is crucial that foster carers and adopters have great patience and a deep understanding about the source of their child's defiance, lying, angry outbursts, isolation, and lack of interest in new experiences. They need to mentally search for the child under the problems and help that child to emerge. They need to remember that the routine act of discipline may be experienced by the child as being abusive. Thus discipline requires clarity, and repetition, all done with an attitude that protects the relationship from the stress of the conflict. This attitude – known as PACE – will be explored shortly.

Sometimes psychological treatment is very beneficial in helping the child to integrate the traumatic experience. After building safety within their relationship, the therapist gently explores the traumatic events, helping the child to recall those events in small parts, taking breaks when necessary. The therapist helps the child to become aware of how he experienced the trauma and to begin to doubt the original meaning of the trauma that was given by the perpetrator. The presence of an emotionally strong and available foster carer or adoptive parent can enable the child to do this integrative work much sooner and faster. The carer's compassionate comforting of the child is likely to produce a sense of safety that the therapist might not be able to create when alone with the child. Comforting by the carer will also help the child to differentiate the carer from the abusive parent, and this will help to integrate the trauma. This process of remembering the event in therapy and developing new meanings for it enables the child to re-experience the event and create a new story about its impact on his life now.

Relational engagement

Since children abused by their parents were violated and betrayed within the most important relationships in their young lives, it is not surprising that they often find it difficult to enter into relationships with their foster carers, adoptive parents, teachers and therapists. They may have difficulty sitting and engaging in mutual interests and activities. They often have great trouble just having a conversation about routine events. They can become uncomfortable with taking turns and sharing. To co-operate with another person means giving up a sense of control and they often cling to control, thinking that it will keep them safe.

The best way to help traumatised children begin to relax their need to control and encourage them to engage in reciprocal conversations is to make them feel safe. The relationship itself can help to generate safety if their caregiver approaches them with acceptance. This is an active stance of welcoming the child, discovering the child and feeling empathy for the child, without judgement or conditions. To assist the child to feel safe enough to engage in these conversations with their parents involves the attitude of **PACE**: being **Playful, Accepting, Curious and Empathic** (Golding and Hughes, 2012).

PACE communicates to your child that you love them for better or for worse. Their special place in your heart is due to who they are rather than whether or not they behave in a "good" way. Using the relationship (never through anger experienced as shaming along with avoidance and threats of separation) helps the child to get through the hard times and to maintain hope that they deserve such a life. It is important that they do not have to earn the time to be with their carers and can have fun without responsibilities.

Playfulness: Finding ways to get back to this light reciprocal enjoyment quickly after a major conflict is one of the more challenging and important aspects of raising a traumatised child. It might be a slow process for both carer and child, but its value must not be forgotten.

Acceptance of the child is crucial when the parent is evaluating the child's behaviour. The child's thoughts, feelings and wishes are accepted completely as being neither right nor wrong, but simply reflecting the child's inner life at that time. The child is then more

17

likely to share them with the parent, and this may prevent him from expressing himself through misbehaviour. Accepting the child's inner life also helps him to have less shame over who he is, and to experience realistic guilt and desire to change specific behaviours.

Within the attitude of acceptance, the parent is able to express unconditional **curiosity** about the meaning of the child's behaviours which, in turn, helps the child to explore with the parent whether a given behaviour is in the best interest of the child and family. These explorations occur with the intent to understand the child's inner life rather than to evaluate the child. The parent lightly wonders: 'Why do you think you did that?' rather than sternly demanding: 'Why did you do that?'

PACE is not complete without **empathy**. Empathy conveys to the child that the parent is with the child in their feelings of distress. The parent both understands the child's experience and feels the emotions associated with it. Empathy creates the safety needed for the child to be vulnerable and to rely on the parent for comfort and guidance. Empathy is not reassurance ('It will get better'), but communicates that the parent is with the child ('That really seems hard for you'). These four traits of PACE enable the child to feel safe enough to explore, with the parent, who he now is and, also, is able to become.

Positive affect enhancement

Just as traumatised children have difficulty regulating negative emotions and their affective expression, they also have difficulty regulating positive emotions and their expression. Excitement, joy, laughter and love often lead to anxiety, sometimes anger and withdrawal. Positive emotions are often experienced as being frightening. There are various reasons for this. Because of his shame, the child might believe that he does not deserve good feelings. He is uncomfortable with sharing happy times out of fear that he will come to want them, only for them to be withdrawn, and he will feel abandoned again. It is better to rely only on himself than to rely on someone who can decide that he is not worth caring for. Also, regulating the full range of emotions requires practice, and this practice works best for infants or toddlers who are engaged positively with parents or carers. Over time, the young child then becomes comfortable with "big emotions" and is less likely to become dysregulated when they are evoked.

CHAPTER **3**

Frequently asked questions

Why is it hard for the child to get over the trauma?

A traumatic event evokes an intense emotion, primarily terror, while the child is experiencing that event. The strength of the emotion makes it very difficult for the child to reflect on what is happening in order to make sense of it and to be able to manage a similar event in the future. Any memories of it evoke the same emotional intensity, so that the memory itself becomes as terrifying as the original event. Other events that are similar to the original trauma also evoke a similar emotional response and activate the original emotion and whatever ways the child found to cope with it in the first place. This is likely to prevent the child from reflecting on the incident and developing more adaptive ways of dealing with it or comparable events in the future.

Isn't it better to encourage the child to forget the trauma and focus on the present, rather than revisit the past?

If the child were able to simply forget the trauma, then it would make sense to focus on the present and ignore it. The difficulty is that the trauma from the past is still active in the child's mind in the present, and is likely to be activated by many similar events. Even if the child is able, at times, to distract herself from the memory of the traumatic event, most likely there will be times when the memory of it intrudes into the child's attention and dysregulates her functioning. Even successful distractions will also interfere with the child giving attention to things that she has to learn at school and in daily life.

Isn't it better to focus on coping skills to manage the trauma, rather than on the emotions associated with the trauma?

Developing coping skills may in fact be a helpful part of the successful treatment of trauma. However, these skills are best developed after first addressing – identifying, reducing and regulating – the intense emotions associated with the trauma. Only then will the child be able to consistently access her reflective skills and begin to use these coping skills.

Won't providing the child with comfort and support regarding the trauma foster dependency and immaturity?

Providing the child with comfort and support regarding her traumatic past will encourage the child to depend upon her caregiver, in order to be able to face and reduce the impact of the trauma. This process will encourage the child to rely upon her caregiver when necessary, and will not foster a general dependency that will prevent the child from developing the parallel skills needed for self-reliance. This is evident in thousands of studies involving attachment research. Children who are securely

21

attached to their caregivers tend to be quite able to rely on themselves as adults, while still relying on their partner or good friends when this is in their best interest.

Children who take comfort from their parents around traumatic events tend to resolve these events more quickly and fully and are then able to proceed with their maturation more successfully than do those children whose attention and energy are directed toward continuously coping with the trauma.

Professionals are trained to work with trauma. If parents discuss the trauma with the child, might that make it worse?

Professionals who are trained to work with trauma might well be helpful in enabling the child to resolve the traumatic event, but consulting with the child's caregiver about the trauma might be the most important element of their work. What the child needs most is a regulated adult who is present with her in her terror as she recalls the trauma, and whose presence itself reduces the intensity of the terror. As the terror is reduced, the adult needs to assist the child in recalling the event, and gradually to make sense of it in a manner that reduces the shame and terror associated with it. The child will then be able to develop confidence that she is now safe and that similar events are not likely to occur in the future, or if they do, she will have the support of an adult in handling it. The comforting presence and the ongoing availability of the child's primary caregiver will create greater confidence than a professional who does not see the child regularly.

Is there a danger that the horrific nature of their child's trauma will cause parents to become too upset to discuss it with their child and so not be helpful?

This danger does exist when the parent first becomes aware of the trauma, or if they become frightened that they will not be able to help their child, or if the trauma activates something from their own history. Because of this, it is wise for parents to speak with professionals alone before the start of their child's treatment. This will enable them to first deal with their own emotions about their child's trauma, to hear the professional's recommendations regarding how best to help their child, and to become aware of any aspects of their own history that might become activated. A few such sessions are often sufficient for parents to be able to assist their child by being present during the course of treatment. If this proves to be too difficult for the parent, it would be best for the child to receive individual treatment.

When alone with their child who has been traumatised, parents should not direct her to explore the past together. They should allow her to initiate and then lead discussion of the trauma, and to end the discussion as soon as she wants to. When a child does take the initiative to discuss the trauma with a parent, the parent should listen intently with empathy, rather than discourage the child from speaking about it.

Is there a danger that by focusing on the child's trauma, it will become an excuse for the child's misbehaviour?

The child's trauma will not become an excuse for misbehaviour unless the caregiver considers it to be an excuse, but it may be the reason for the misbehaviour, and therefore might guide the parent to help the child to handle behavioural expectations more successfully. This might include changing the expectations or providing more structure and supportive presence in order to aid the child in managing her responsibilities.

Should the parent initiate discussion of the trauma if the child does not, or wait as long as necessary for the child to do so?

The initial position of the parent might best be to wait, while being present and available to discuss the trauma whenever the child wants to do so. This could include times that are inconvenient for the parent and it may seem like the child is using this tactic to avoid what she does not want to do. However, a situation that involves separation from the parent – going to bed, going to school – might have activated the traumatic memory, and the child's motive for bringing it up at this point is best understood in that light.

If the child is struggling with her daily functioning or is showing other signs of distress seemingly related to the trauma, the parent would be wise to initiate the discussion at some point. This should be done tentatively ('I wonder if you might be struggling with…') and in a general way ('What happened must have been really hard on you and I wonder if it is on your mind a lot...').

Should it be the goal for the traumatised child to move from being a victim to being a survivor?

Being a survivor implies that the impact of the trauma is now less than it was initially, when the daily functioning of the child primarily reflected their being a victim of the trauma. A child survivor is demonstrating that the trauma has not prevented her from moving forward again with her routine activities and developmental achievements.

While the first goal is to move from being a victim to being a survivor, a further goal is for the child to be able to develop a sense of self that is much deeper and more comprehensive than that of a survivor. Following the trauma, the child's identity needs to become formed by many other diverse experiences and relationships, which, over time, will greatly reduce the impact of the trauma. The child is not defined primarily by the trauma, but it may lead to various strengths and vulnerabilities in the child's future, which do not limit the quality of life that the child is able to attain.

24

CHAPTER 4

Specific parenting tasks

Establish safety

When your child has experienced trauma, your primary task is to help them to re-establish their sense of safety in their day-to-day life. As has been said throughout this book, being and feeling safe is crucial for your child's overall emotional, cognitive, social, psychological and physical development. When children – or adults too, for that matter – do not experience a sense of safety in the present time and place, they are likely to devote so much of their time and energy to attaining or preserving a precarious sense of safety that they have little time for pursuing their other developmental tasks, including learning about the world (Hughes, 2009).

Ensure external safety

Your child needs to know, and possibly be given the information again and again, that the source of the trauma is no longer present.

Whether it was a dog, a person or an accident, your child needs to understand what steps have been taken to make him safe now. You may not be able to guarantee that a similar event will not happen again, but you can give various reasons to help your child to trust that you have taken every possible measure to prevent its recurrence. Many repetitions over weeks, months or even years may be necessary before the traumatic event is no longer impacting on your child's daily attention and activities.

To help your child to feel safe in his environment, he is likely to benefit from a high degree of predictability. Thus, there should be clear routines, with schedules and structure, so that he will know what is happening throughout the day. This will include anticipating with confidence that the details, the people and the sequence will not vary without him knowing in advance the reasons for any changes and your confidence that he will still be safe.

Your child will also benefit from knowing that you, or someone else that your child is safe with, is nearby in case there is any unforeseen problem. He should know that he can ask for help at any time and that help will be provided. He does not have to convince anyone that he needs it. He asks, and it will be provided without questions. Depending upon his age, your availability by mobile phone may suffice, but he has to be certain that you will answer it immediately if he calls.

When there are new events or changes in routines, you need to be available to be with him the first few times to help him to become comfortable with them.

When your child expresses fears about anything in his environment, respond first with PACE. Accept his fear, be curious about it, have empathy for it (it is unlikely at that moment that being playful will help him). Only after you believe that you really understand his experience, and that he trusts that you understand, do you then give him information, reassurance and/or a strategy to manage the fear alone or with you. Then you listen to his response and again respond with PACE so that he trusts that you really understand his objection, and then respond again with a variation on how to manage the fear.

Facilitate internal safety

One of the reasons we tend to underestimate the impact of psychological trauma is that we often do not see physical signs of the trauma. We think – though we might not say it – 'It's all in your head', as if that indicates that it should be easy to make it go away. We want to believe that if he just doesn't think about it, or if he distracts himself, or thinks about other things, it will fade away. Or the opposite – if he *does* think about it, comes to grips with it, does not let it get in the way, or gets over it, it will fade away. As if one small – partially developed in children – area of the brain that works best when we feel safe, could instruct the other areas of the brain as to what they need to do – and that those areas will listen. The areas of the brain that specialise in threats to safety, that work best when in danger, are not likely to listen to areas of the brain that only work well when you are safe. Telling your child to forget it and to get over it is very likely to fail and may well make the problem worse by generating more hopelessness, shame and isolation because he knows he cannot do what you tell him he can do.

You have to help your child to be safe – in his mind too, not just in his external world. He will not be safe if something seemingly insignificant in the external world – a sound, a smell, a TV show, a tone of voice of someone in the market, a sensation in his body – activates the terror of the trauma, almost as intensely as the trauma itself. He needs to be safe in his own mind, so that when it wanders into, or is awakened, in areas of the brain that contain traumatic memories, he will remain safe, even if distressed by the memories. He will then remain confident that he can manage or can get your help to manage those memories without re-experiencing the trauma.

How can you help him to be safe in his own mind? First, when he shows any signs of being frightened by something in his mind, you have to be emotionally strong, present, confident and comforting for him. You are available for him to tell you what he is thinking, feeling, remembering, though you do not insist that he does so. You accept the presence of those features of his mind – they are present – and you are communicating that you will be with him as long as they are, and as long as he needs you to be. You are present to co-regulate his emotions, whether they are terror, despair and/or shame, and your emotions are regulated in the background, with him having no fear that he is a burden to you, which is too much for you, or that he has to support you. When with him, you need to be one hundred per cent focused on meeting whatever he needs from you. Later, when he is not present, you focus on your own needs, ideally with the support of someone who can be strong for you.

When you are with him, focus first on whatever emotions he is experiencing. He needs to not be afraid that they will be too much for him – or you – to manage. He needs not to be ashamed of them or believe that they make him a baby, and he needs to experience your confidence that his emotions are not too much for him – especially with your presence for now – to handle.

If he shows an energy to talk, though it is hard, have gentle, open-ended questions to help him with the process, to give him confidence that you are interested, believe him, and will be able to understand the event while helping him to understand it. Later, in that meeting or the next or the next, he may begin to wonder about the big picture – why it happened, why a person traumatised him (if it was a person), was it his fault, will it happen again, will other people know about it, what will they think about it and him, and how will it affect him in the future. Embedded in that will be what you think about what happened: was it his fault, and is he now broken, damaged and ruined forever because of what happened? Your response will greatly influence his experience of this in the short term and possibly the long term. If you believe that he will never recover from the trauma, he is likely to believe that as well and that will make his recovery more difficult. If you believe that it was terrifying for him, and very hard, and that with your presence and those of others, and his resilience and other strengths, he will recover, he is more likely to do so. He is working out without conscious thought whether or not he will be a victim, a survivor, or a child who was traumatised and who also will be a strong, loving, clever, popular, and capable person. Maybe he will wobble for a while, but only for a while. Your confidence will become his confidence.

And gradually it gets trickier to know what he needs. His mind is likely to slowly begin to notice the life outside and available to him now that the traumatic events have ceased. The acuteness of the traumatic memories is less and the draw of healthy activities is greater. Does he need a bit more focus on safety and predictability or should he be encouraged to explore the world again? More healing time or time to move on? Probably both, but what is the best mix?

Your best first response is probably to give him the safety to wonder about today and tomorrow and to introduce some change. Stay with PACE, give some information about small steps, show him the ability to change his mind, and the possibility of changing some things that he has done before so that they might be more manageable now. Show in your attitude that if he tries and it does not work, it is not a failure as much as gaining knowledge about what a better next step – and when to take it – might actually be. But still comfort him over his disappointment.

Suppose in waiting for him to make the initial choice, he seems frozen, too afraid to choose? And it goes on that way. Stay with PACE. And then with confidence, say (after much thought): 'Well, this is what I'd like us to do tomorrow. It might be hard, I'll be right with you the whole way, and then we'll talk about how it went afterwards. Would you rather go at 10am or 11am? Rather wear your blue outfit or red?' Your momentum, comfort and confidence may give him the strength to do it with you. While being frozen, he may have known that he needed you to decide and though he frets, he may be relieved. Of course, when the time comes to do it, you cannot force it, he cannot be trapped, and you have to respond to it not happening, with PACE. Again, it is a source of new knowledge for the future, not a failure.

Remember that with your strength, confidence and love, you can walk with your traumatised child, lead him from the rain into the sun, from winter into spring. Through the healing power of unconditional comfort, patience, care and safety, he will begin to want to laugh and play and argue and even say 'no'. And whatever he enjoyed in the past, he will notice he is enjoying those same friends and activities again. He might check in a lot. He might also be confused about what he wants. He may be more oppositional or clinging, or both, than he ever was before. He may demonstrate a week or a month or two showing nothing but "healthy childhood behaviours" and you find yourself thinking that the nightmare is over. And then he has a hard day, an unexpected fright, an experience of shame, and he falls back into fears and shame and doubt. You may be tempted to try to pull him out of it, to insist that he let it go. You may want to remind him of the past few weeks or months. Don't. Stay with PACE. Healing is cyclical and though the hard memories, thoughts and feelings are less frequent and intense, it is unlikely that they will disappear, without returning, here and there. Sometimes you will know why, sometimes you won't. Remain patient and confident and he will resume his journey back to his experience of safety, success and his childhood.

Teach your child to trust

This is not as easy as it might sound. When a child has not been traumatised by their parent, they have an assumption that they are able to trust their motives even when they disagree with the parent's decision. When a child *has* been traumatised by their parent, that child does not have an assumption that the parent's motives involve his best interest. Rather, that child has a negative assumption that the parent either does not care what is best for him or actually wants to hurt him or make him unhappy. Building trust involves helping the child to move from this negative assumption to the positive one involving his best interests.

How to go about it?

- Set limits around the child's challenging behaviours, without having negative assumptions about the child's motives.

- After a conflict, or break in the relationship for whatever reason, be ready and able to repair the relationship. *Demonstrate that the relationship is more important than any conflict.*

- Respond quickly to your child's expressions of wants or needs, but also initiate activities with him. You relate with him not just when he seeks you out. You seek him out because being with him is special to you.

- Help him to be aware that you think of him when you are not together. Say, 'At work today, I was thinking about what you said'. Pick up something for him while shopping that reminded you of him.

- Acknowledge and accept his disappointment or annoyance when you say "no" to him. You do feel sad that it is hard for him at times when you have to say "no" because you think it is in his best interests.

Protect your readiness to care

Raising a child is hard work, and raising a traumatised child who has various developmental challenges caused by the trauma is harder still. When we attempt to raise a child who does not respond to our care, we – all parents – are at risk of finding it difficult to provide care in a consistent, ongoing way. Intimate relationships, whether they be relationships between partners or between parent and child, are designed neurologically to work in a reciprocal manner. When the child does not respond to the parent's care, the parent is at risk of developing "blocked care" (Hughes and Baylin, 2012). You need to protect your readiness to maintain what can often be difficult, *ongoing care*.

How to go about it?

- Remember that providing care is a marathon, not a sprint. You need to pace yourself, replenish your sources of energy, accept the wobbles and need for breaks, and stay focused on the distant horizon.

- Caring for yourself so that you are able to consistently care for your child begins with having someone (or some two) care for you when you need it. Be clear what you need from your partner, if you have one. The same applies to your best friend, sibling, mentor or fellow parent. Receive from others in order to be able to give to your child for the long haul.

- What are your sources of satisfaction, peace and joy apart from your identity as a parent and partner? Be sure to leave time for those activities in your daily, or at least weekly, life.

- Remember that you will make mistakes. You are not a robot or saint; accept them and learn from them. If you go into shame when you make a mistake, you are more likely to blame your child for it and do it again.

● Reflect on your strengths and the challenges that you have overcome as a parent. During tough times you are likely to devalue your strengths and exaggerate your vulnerabilities. List your strengths and remember not to judge your skills as a parent based solely on whether or not your child is benefiting from them here and now. Sometimes you will do your very best and it will not seem to help your child.

● Remember that there is no way of knowing whether even the most difficult situation is hopeless. Many times, after months and even years of very challenging behaviour, a child, a teenager or young adult finally emerges into a life of satisfaction and success. Often, this child/young adult will say to their parents, 'You never gave up on me. Even when you told me to leave home when I was 18 because I was stealing from you and bringing drugs home, I knew that you didn't want to send me away. You still loved me.'

Note the trauma of absence

Neglect tends to cause more psychological and developmental problems than specific acts of abuse. Neglect says: 'You are not special to me. You are not lovable. There is something wrong with you and I do not want to be with you.' The neglected child is not looked at with loving eyes, is not held or touched with affection, comfort or delight, and he does not have a place in his parent's mind and heart. While your child might trust that you will not abuse him, he might well have a harder time trusting that you will love him and not forget him.

What to do about it?

- Be understanding and patient over his desire to be with you a great deal. Realise that his dependency does not represent a fear of growing up as much as a need to establish a sense of self through his relationship with you that is necessary for him to grow up well. Think toddler, regardless of his age.

- Organise your home so that there is work and play space for your child in the main living areas where you frequently are, rather than in his bedroom or in a play room.

- Schedule some times each day when doing something with your child is your top priority. Be predictable and only cancel for emergencies.

- Schedule some "alone time" for yourself, being clear that it is something you need, not because you want to get away from him. Have something for him to do while you have your private time and have something planned to do with him when your time is over.

- Be sure to have him contribute to family rituals. Be sure that he is in family photos placed about the house. Exchange special keepsakes that will remind you of each other when you are not together.

- Make sure that he has a life story book with both a story and pictures, and with plenty of space to add to it, starting from his first day in your house.

Creating the opportunity for competence and joy

Trauma is not to be minimised or denied. Nor need it be ever present in the child's mind so that he dwells on it and anticipates its recurrence, vigilantly, for years. External and internal safety enables the child to set the trauma aside and direct his mind and spirit toward catching up with his developmental challenges and opportunities and actively become engaged with living again.

To take advantage of his opportunities for a good life after his traumatic past, he needs to discover his personal qualities and strengths that were not seen and valued when he was living in his traumatic past. He needs you to discover these traits with him and then to express your experience of him. You need to find qualities such as courage, resilience, persistence, honesty, compassion, creativity, cleverness, loyalty, and optimism, so that he will know that those qualities are aspects of who he is. He has a great deal to contribute to your family, community and the world.

How to do this?

- Your discoveries are not judgements but spontaneous expressions of delight or pride over his motives and actions. Just feed back your experience without adding any "take-home-message".

- If your positive reactions to him seem to cause him to be anxious, tone them down a bit and reflect with him that you understand how your view of him might make him somewhat uncomfortable because it is new to him, and he might fear that you will eventually be disappointed in him or expect him to be perfect.

- If he is hesitant to take advantage of opportunities provided, don't push them, and simply leave them available for him, ready if and when he decides to pursue them.

- As he becomes more comfortable with his new life, he is still likely to have hard times when he seems to return to the thoughts, feelings and behaviours associated with his past. Accept these episodes rather than becoming frustrated by them. Do not actively encourage him to forget his past and to focus only on his life now. He will not forget his past, nor would it be best for him to do so if he could. The person he is today and in the future will always be influenced, in part, by his past. He needs to understand it and integrate it rather than deny it. At times, this process will hold his attention in the past. Be with him then, listening and comforting and understanding, rather than trying to pull him away from it.

- Express gratitude to him for who he is – all of him – and how he has added to your family. You certainly have given him a lot, while at the same time he has given you a lot too. Be aware of that and help him to be aware of it too. He has contributed to the meaning and happiness of good people – his new family – something that he had never thought would be possible when he was living amidst the trauma.

CHAPTER 5

How the child might be affected at different stages of development

Preschool

Pre-school children are still in the process of developing their affect regulation and reflective functioning skills, so when they are traumatised, these abilities can be easily disrupted. They are therefore likely to show the impact of the trauma within all of their major areas of functioning – emotional, social, cognitive, physical. New skills may disappear and they will regress to a prior level of functioning. The four-year-old now seems like she was when she was three or two, and what is more, she seems like an unhappy younger child. She is probably more clingy than other children of her age, not tolerating short separations or having her mind somewhere else (e.g. playing with a phone or watching TV). Her speech and language development tend to be delayed; her appetite, sleep and toilet training are affected. When first placed with a new carer, this child is likely to show behavioural extremes, which could range from aggressive outbursts to sitting, staring and rocking. She may be rigidly "good" for a period of time, until she has a sense of whether she will be abused or abandoned if she misbehaves. Then she might move toward the challenging, disruptive extreme.

School age

Even for securely attached children, beginning or changing school can create anxiety over the extensive separation from their caregivers. Traumatised children are focused a great deal on feeling safe and they may have particular difficulty being separated from their caregivers for the hours that make up the school day. Many foster children function better at home, in large part because of the proximity to their caregivers.

Children who have been traumatised are also at risk of having difficulty attending to their academic tasks (Bomber and Hughes, 2013). Intrusive thoughts and feelings secondary to the trauma may make it hard for them to concentrate on their assignments. Also, if they are hypervigilant regarding possible threats in the external world, their attention to their school work is likely to be limited. Since developmental trauma can have pervasive effects on children, there may be delays and gaps in their overall cognitive functioning and skill level. If, because of their traumatic history, their overall developmental age has been compromised, there is a definite risk that the academic expectations being made are too high. This mistake is most often made about traumatised children because they may be very inconsistent in their functional level. One day they function at their general level of ability and the next day, if the impact of their traumatic history is greater, their functioning is compromised. Regretfully, this is often seen as a motivational problem (i.e. she did it on Tuesday, so she can do it, she's just not trying today). This variable pattern of functioning is common in the recovery period from trauma, but it is often not recognised.

Teenage years

The teen years are likely to be somewhat volatile at the best of times, and traumatised teenagers are at risk from more extreme emotions, including terror, despair and rage. These could be related to the trauma directly as well as to problems with their overall affect regulation skills, which may be a secondary effect of their traumatic history. Their struggles to manage these strong emotions sometimes culminate in behavioural outbursts, which can include harming themselves or others.

Teenagers generally struggle with issues of maturation and independence. The teenager who has experienced developmental trauma may have general difficulty relying on her foster carers or adoptive parents. She may have developed a rigid self-reliance that prevents her from turning to her carers for guidance in dealing with the increased challenges of adolescence. Relying on their carers is even more difficult for young people who have experienced multiple placements.

The impact of the trauma may also become more intense because teenagers tend to have an increased ability to reflect, and therefore to have a greater desire to make sense of their lives in order to begin to develop a more coherent life story. When they have been traumatised by their parents, they may experience even more acutely during their adolescence how their trust in their parents was violated. This may be very difficult for them to make sense of and may cause them to be even more pessimistic about their future.

CHAPTER **6**

Educational and social issues

Education

Developmental trauma places the child at risk of challenges to their overall cognitive functioning, including their ability to learn. Related challenges might be to speech and language development, auditory processing, sensory integration, and general ability to concentrate. As the academic demands increase over the years, these challenges might become more severe if they have not been adequately addressed within specialised educational services.

Even if their learning abilities seem intact, traumatised children may not be able to focus consistently on their academic functioning because of their ongoing experience of threat, their emotional volatility, and their sense of despair, which can overwhelm them with a feeling of hopelessness (Bomber and Hughes, 2013). Being unmotivated is often superficially judged as a choice that they have made and have the power to change, which is very often not so. Motivation, like most functions of our brains, is not something that is under our conscious control. Or, it might be more accurate to say, that some superficial wishes we can choose to make happen, while other deeper goals are much more determined by core brain systems that we might be aware of, but not be able to turn on and off.

Social issues

Inter-personal trauma is very likely to have an impact on our subsequent inter-personal relationships. Since developmental trauma represents a betrayal within the original, primary relationship, future relationships will probably be lacking in trust. Many children, being traumatised by their parents, are likely to re-enact that loss of control and habitually adopt a submissive attitude in their future relationships. They tend to work hard to please their foster carers and are overly "good" or "manipulative" or seem to live as chameleons who constantly change themselves to please other people. It provides them with a semblance of safety: if they are liked, they will not be hurt. Other children take the opposite path in their attempt to be safe: they try to dominate others and are quite oppositional and aggressive towards their carers, while they bully their peers. Either path shows an inability to engage others in reciprocal relationships, in which neither is in control but each is relating in a co-operative manner, taking turns, and enjoying each other's presence. Lacking reciprocity in their relationships with peers, it is hard for them to have a best friend, unless one person in the friendship is dominant and the other is submissive. They are unlikely to welcome the vulnerability or to be comfortable with the experiences of empathy and comfort that best friends evoke.

As children who experience developmental trauma become teenagers, they may have great difficulty with relationships that involve emotional and sexual intimacy. Such a degree of intimacy can arouse a semblance of the intimacy of the parent–child relationship. If a young person has been sexually abused by a parent or substitute parent, sexual intimacy is likely to activate any unresolved thoughts or feelings associated with the abuse.

CHAPTER 7

Conclusion

Trauma and resilience

It is important to remember that trauma – even when a child is traumatised by their own parents – does not mean that the child's life is ruined. Human beings, both children and adults, have the capacity to be resilient, to overcome obstacles, to become stronger in the face of adversity, to become fully functioning adults not only in spite of having been traumatised, but sometimes, in part, due to the trauma itself.

Resilience tends to become stronger when a child has had an adult to whom she is able to turn for safety and new learning about self and the world. Securely attached individuals tend to become resilient individuals. While providing the appropriate treatment for a traumatised child may be an important part of the child's healing and continuing development, providing that child with a caregiver to whom she is able to become securely attached is more important.

A coherent narrative

One of the most damaging effects of a child being traumatised, especially when the result is developmental trauma, is that it makes it difficult for the child to develop an integrated sense of self and a coherent autobiographical narrative. These are both characteristics of a securely attached child and adult. Attachment security facilitates a child's ability to manage a full range of stressful events through developing both reflective and emotional competency. These skills enable the child to resolve and integrate past traumas while managing future stressors so that they are less likely to become traumatic.

Strong families often prove to be stronger than past traumas. Parents must never forget that their traumatised child needs them to feel safe, to develop confidence and joy, and to discover their own abilities and their worth. Parents must also remember that their traumatised child needs them to discover who she or he is, along with who he or she has the potential to become; who your child was born to be, and now has the possibility of becoming, because you are your child's parent.

Years ago, in my efforts to convey the effects of developmental trauma and the extreme difficulty it is for children traumatised by their own parents to begin to trust their new foster carers or adoptive parents, I wrote a number of poems about both the trauma and the journey of trust and self-discovery, which were then published. The following is one of them, along with a brief description of it, both reproduced from *It Was That One Moment: Dan Hughes' poetry and reflections on a life of making relationships with children, young people and their families* (2012), with the kind permission of Worth Publishing Ltd.

One of the most damaging aspects of abuse and neglect is that it reduces one's openness to establishing a relationship with an adult, a relationship which is crucial in discovering who one is, and how one is able to have a positive influence on another. A child's worth is greatly impaired by the abuse itself. Then, if the child is exposed to a relationship with a caring person, he is less likely to be open to that relationship, even though he is very unlikely to change his negative, poorly defined sense of self without having such a relationship. Inter-subjectivity is the primary source of our social and emotional sense of self and it is greatly compromised when a child has been abused by the first individuals with whom he tried to have such an inter-subjective experience.

In this poem I attempted to emphasise how difficult it was for the child to be open to the positive experience that her adoptive mother had of her. Once she was able to be consistently open to such an experience – with a mother who saw her worth, who experienced what was of value about her – then she would be able to benefit from such experiences and re-experience her sense of self.

Dancing in the Light

Her name was Katie
and her name, along with her birth,
her face, and her voice—her cries,
murmurs, and grasping breaths –
were given to her as a curse to life,
leaving her clutching hypervigilance
if she still wanted to breathe.

Alone she lived,
her mind and heart clinging to
solitary connections and beats.
When Jackie entered her life,
this new mother was rejected as

45

any foreign body should be if
the organism is to live.

Mothers were sharks
ruthlessly waiting while circling for
the mind's energy and the heart's blood.

Fighting sharks may well seem hopeless
but Katie did fight with Jackie
for there seemed to be no other way
to survive.
Until that time when
Jackie ceased to be a shark
and Katie ceased to see herself as a curse.

Jackie did circle for Katie's
mind and heart,
A gentle, persistent, search.
With a face of compassion
A voice of continuous welcome
A touch of strong safety.

It was that one moment,
one similar to thousands of prior moments.
When Katie began to sense,
to know,
to feel – felt in those parts of her
that had never been felt before.

That one moment when Katie knew –
When she dared to know –
When she leaped into her knowing –
that Jackie was discovering some
parts of her, parts
that were gifts to the world,

that needed to be named by her,
to be cherished by her,
to be experienced with
delight and joy
and awe and love...
by her.
Just as they were experienced
by her mother.

And at this point,
When time seems to circle back upon itself.
Katie sees Jackie seeing her seeing Jackie.
She knows that her mind and heart –
actively joining with Jackie's –
will explode in celebrations.
Will beat in rhythms of life
that have moved for mystical generations
from mothers to daughters to mothers again,
dancing in the light.

References

Cook A, Spinazzola J, Ford J, Lanktree C, Blaustein M, Sprague C, Cloitre M, DeRosa R, Hubbard R, Kagen R, Liautaud J, Mallah K, Olafson E and van der Kolk B (2005) 'Complex trauma in children and adolescents', *Psychiatric Annals*, 35:5, pp 390–398

Bomber L and Hughes DA (2013) *Settling to Learn: Why relationships matter in school*, London: Worth Publishing

Golding KS and Hughes D (2012) *Creating Loving Attachments*, London: Jessica Kingsley Publishers

Hughes D (2009) *Attachment-Focused Parenting*, New York, NY: WW Norton

Hughes D (2012) *It Was That One Moment: Dan Hughes' poetry and reflections on a life of making relationships with children, young people, and their families*, London: Worth Publishing Ltd

Hughes D and Baylin J (2012) *Brain-Based Parenting: The neuroscience of caregiving for healthy attachment*, New York, NY: WW Norton

PARENTING A CHILD AFFECTED BY CHILDHOOD TRAUMA

MATTHEW BLYTHE

The early years

Tom was born at 14.37. He came out screaming. He was cross; he wasn't ready to come out yet. Four minutes later James came out. He was quiet, unresponsive, floppy. The midwife and doctor worked on him. He screamed as he took his first breath. He was taken to special care so they could keep an eye on him. Tom spent a short time with his mother, and then he too was taken away to be with his brother, whilst their mother's caesarean section was sewn up. The nurses were still trying to contact the babies' father.

The family spent nearly a week in hospital. Mum was slow to recover and was finding it difficult to look after the two babies. The family was already known to social services. Mum, who had learning difficulties, had a child from a previous relationship. She had found looking after her three-year-old daughter a real challenge. The

boys' father also had learning difficulties, compounded
by addictive tendencies to gambling, drinking, smoking
and cannabis. He found taking medication to control his
epilepsy difficult, so was often found unconscious after a
seizure.

The newly-expanded family lived in a small two-bedroom
rented house. They had very little support from their
extended family – relationships with grandparents were
volatile. Chaos quickly spiralled. Professional support
was put in place; health care workers flagged up their
concerns. The parents saw the professionals as a threat,
and intrusive.

Then there was the house fire. The house was gutted.
Everyone got out safely, but the house was destroyed.
The family had to move when Tom and James were
around two or three months old. They moved out of the
area, and found another house to rent. The professionals
tried to support them, but caseloads were not
transferred in time, so support lagged behind the family's
needs. The father's health deteriorated. He became
more dependent on cannabis; both parents were getting
more and more angry with each other. The professionals
became more involved, and the children were placed on
the "at risk" register.

One night, feeling under pressure, the family moved
out of their home, leaving most of their possessions
behind. They moved to yet another new area. Again the
professionals had to play "catch up". This time, the police
were the first to be involved. Reports of screaming and
shouting were heard by neighbours and the father was
taken into custody overnight. Things calmed down for
a time and the family accepted the support they were

offered. The twins were now getting more mobile and were often controlled by being strapped into their double buggy to allow their mum some peace and quiet.

One day, the health visitor called in to see the family and she found the twins in the backyard, strapped into their buggy, in direct sunlight. Both were burning in the midday sun. They were taken to hospital but allowed back home the next day. A week later the bath was left running, causing the house to flood. The family moved once more.

When the police caught up with the family again, they arrested the father for aggravated assault against the mother. She then moved to be back near her family, but her family were not supportive.

The twins' mother soon found herself in a new relationship, with another controlling, violent man, who had recently been released from prison. The boys were now around two years old. The new partner brought more chaos to the family. Unsavoury people were invited to the house; there was a constant stream of unknown adult visitors. It is still uncertain exactly what happened during this period, but the mother, her partner and the three children moved a couple more times. Surprisingly, the authorities de-escalated their concerns and reduced the level of support for the family. The adults were compliant and things on the surface were calmer. One week later, having being left with unknown adults, James was injured and the children were immediately taken into care.

James stayed in hospital for six weeks whilst his leg healed; Tom and their sister went to live with a foster carer. The boys must have experienced this as a horrific event: they were separated, James was hospitalised, and Tom was sent to live with strangers. They had not done anything wrong – and they were only three years old. They must have been totally bewildered and frightened. All that they knew, no matter how bad it had been, was taken away in an instant. They continued to see their mother under the supervision and scrutiny of social workers.

Then the boys got lucky; they stayed together with the same foster carer for three years. They had stability, they had each other and their sister. But she moved to a different placement after two years, creating more upheaval and confusion for the twins. They would now only see their sister whenever the professionals organised it.

Unfortunately, the foster carer placed few boundaries around the already chaotic boys. Although it was a nurturing home, they were often left to their own devices and allowed to run amok around the large house. They were frequently late for school and engagement with the school was poor. There was talk about moving them to another foster home, but it was difficult to find families for older siblings. Three years into their placement I appeared.

I was single. I had a steady job – I worked in health care; I had experience of looking after children; and a good support network of family and friends. I had a small, but nice house. Due to my circumstances, I was looking for school age children so that I could continue to work full time.

The adoption process was very intense, and sometimes

quite intrusive, but I always knew it would be, so that was fine – the social workers needed to know all about me. I went to panel and was approved. It was very soon after approval that the details of the boys were sent to me. I had always wanted a sibling group, two to me sounded easier. They were described as "lively, boisterous twins". This was their last chance for adoption; if it failed, they would be placed in long-term foster care. I was aware that the boys had experienced some upheaval during their time with their birth family but I was never really told about the trauma they had experienced. Certainly I was never warned of the deep-rooted impact this would have on them for years to come.

Things needed to move along quickly as the social workers wanted to move the boys from their current foster placement. During my initial assessment, one of the questions I was asked was: 'What couldn't you cope with?' I still to this day don't know the answer to that – some of the things I have coped with, I would never have thought possible.

The introduction period – the times when I first met the boys – was protracted and fraught. I carried on working, right up to the day they moved in. The introductions lasted three weeks. The first week I went to the foster carer's home. That was awkward, uncomfortable and surreal for me. I felt the whole experience was irritating for the foster carers, and for the boys it must have been bewildering. They had always known they would move somewhere, but they had lived in the same place for several years, they knew the routines, the people, they were part of a family. Then suddenly some bloke appeared and they were going to live with him forever. I did feel for them. The second week was spent learning

SECTION II

their routines, taking them to school, occasional trips to my house. The third week we were completely exhausted. They spent a couple of nights at my house, they then flitted to school and back to the foster carers. It was a really uncomfortable time for everyone.

The boys moved in one March Monday morning. I remember it vividly. The foster carer had been sending black bin bags with their belongings during introductions. Their bedrooms were full already. The car was crammed again with more black bin bags of old clothes, broken toys and clutter. Just clutter. There were no photos. Three years were squashed tightly into ripping bin bags. It seemed to take forever to sort through the jumble: to ascertain what was sentimental, what was precious, what held memories… Very little, it seemed.

On that March morning, the three of us sat in the kitchen. We had biscuits and a drink. The house was silent. The boys looked at each other. James asked why they hadn't got a mum. Tom replied, 'We don't need a mum, we are fine together. We are a team.' The boys were wearing exactly the same clothes – their foster carer thought they looked cute that way. I asked the boys if they wanted to wear the same, or to choose their own clothes. Their own, they decided. They had always wanted to look different from each other, but were not allowed. They were physically identical. They had exactly the same start in life. They had seen the same things and experienced the same events. But they had their own quirks, their own mannerisms and habits. They were totally and utterly unique individuals.

Primary years

When they moved in the boys were feral. Time has blurred how I remember that period, but I do know that we were exhausted ALL of the time. Life just took on a whole new chaos: routines around the boys, meetings with social workers, meetings at school. They demanded my attention from dawn till dusk. Literally. They would wake in the summer at 03.40, and not stop until the sun went down. Blackout blinds were the first thing I fitted. At least we could try to get some sleep. They would run everywhere. I learnt quickly always to keep them in front of me, Tom would invariably run ahead. Head down, running as fast as he could. James would wander, stop and ponder. Sometimes, he would stop and look at something in the middle of the road. So we would hold hands. We would have the three steps rule, never any further than three steps away from me. Always with the sole mission to get somewhere where one could run as fast as he could and the other could stop and stare.

I thought school would offer me some respite, but I was so wrong. I had suggested to the teachers that as the boys were behind academically, maybe they should go down a year so they could try to catch up. The school did not like the idea at all, but soon changed their mind – two weeks after the boys started. The teachers tried to work with me and the twins, but their behaviour was too challenging. Tom found school the most frightening. He would often try to run away. For him it was full of shouting, rules, regulations, but mostly full of fear. He would be hyper alert. Strategies put in place by the teachers were soon given up on because they were not working. Tom was often excluded from lessons, stopped from going on trips. To him (and me) it was a very hostile place. I was given unsought advice all the time, usually in front of Tom. I always felt the school blamed me for Tom's behaviour. They could not and would not listen to advice. They were not consistent with their approaches. New strategies were tried for a short time, and then dismissed as soon as something went wrong. The school's focus was always punitive, focusing on all the things that had gone wrong, instead of building on the positives. I felt that very few of the staff actually liked Tom. In contrast, they thought James was a model pupil, and compared him constantly to Tom. Interestingly, James would contain himself at school, but then overflow with his pent up emotions when he got home. The teachers would never believe me when I tried to tell them what was happening. Tom, James and I look back at that time with a lot of sadness.

I was advised to go on a parenting course, a basic parenting course. I joined a group of parents who were attending because they too were experiencing problems at home. We learnt about "time out", sticker charts, and the "naughty step". These things, I would soon find out, are an absolute "no-no" for children who have experienced early trauma. Punishment and sanctions heightened the boys' fears and anxieties. Their behaviour would explode into violence against me if I just mentioned "time out". I soon learnt that, as much as they were trying to push me away, they had to stay close to me in order to keep themselves safe. I did once send Tom to his room for misbehaving; luckily I caught him as his legs were going out of his bedroom window. In his head, I, like all other adults, had rejected him.

Our social worker did get me onto a course about attachment, which was invaluable. Out went the sticker charts; in came empathy, A LOT of empathy. I became like Sherlock Holmes, trying to deduce why certain things evoked certain reactions. I became a trigger sleuth. Bits of the jigsaw were slotting into place. The edge pieces first, then the more complicated ones. The sky section of our jigsaw is still proving difficult; we keep trying a piece in different places, leaving it, and seeing if something else works better.

Shopping was unbelievable. A supermarket would explode their heads. The first time we went for a "big shop" I lost them both in seconds. The security guards were great and Tom was tracked doing time trials around the frozen section. James was found, eventually, under a display cabinet playing with a toy car. The foster carer said never to take them shopping. It was too hard work, always do online shopping. I decided that this was going to be my challenge. They would need to shop when they were older. So we started slowly. I would do the main shop when they were at school. We would then go and get two or three things at a time. They were sent off on missions, to locate the bananas or milk. ALWAYS IN MY SIGHT. Always a game. Then we could pay and go.

As the missions became bigger, the tension would rise and the behaviour would escalate. I was known to do a toddler tantrum, jumping up and down like in the TV advert, never to mock them, but to distract. I would also abandon the trolley with the shopping, and we would leave, saying we will try again another time. When we actually did manage to do some shopping, I would praise them and point out that we had achieved our mission of purchasing a loaf of bread AND a bottle of milk. Maybe next time we could get the margarine as well. The nice things were always chosen last, as some sort of reward. They soon learnt that chaos meant no biscuits. There was the time though, when Tom had climbed on top of the freezers in a supermarket, shouting for James who had gone missing. I yelled at him to get down, found James and frog-marched them to the car…with them both screaming for the abandoned biscuits…

Meeting up with friends was another challenge. James would sit on anyone's knee. He would stroke their hair or face. He would cling around their necks; he knew no boundaries. I tried not to use the word, but he did manipulate people. He would be utterly endearing; maybe he thought that if he controlled them, he would be safe. It was difficult to tell people not to hug him back or to encourage him. People like hugs. I got my friends to give a quick hug to greet him, then stand up, and peel him off. Tom would hug too, but he was much more boisterous. He would put both his arms around people's necks and squeeze. I don't think he was trying to hurt, but I think he too was trying to control everyone to keep himself safe. I got people to say to him, 'No arms around the neck, we like proper hugs around the waist'.

We tried initially to keep in touch with the foster carers. I had always wanted to, and I always felt it would be positive for the boys. But it seemed to confuse them; every time they spoke on the telephone they would get more unsettled and agitated. They were confused about whether they were going back. It was really hard for the foster carers too, as they had built a very close bond with the boys, but keeping in touch was proving traumatic for the twins. I did try to send Christmas cards and birthday cards for a time, but it was never reciprocated, and the boys wanted to move on.

It was agreed that we would have letterbox contact with the birth family annually. I always ask the boys if they want to write; they never do. I see if they want to ask any questions; they rarely do. The timeframe for the letters means that, if we do actually get a reply, the boys have forgotten what they asked originally. We did for some years meet up with their sister, which the boys really enjoyed, but that stopped when she became an adult and left foster care. We sometimes have a letter from her. The boys do miss her.

Food was a huge issue. They both regressed when they arrived. They could not use a knife and fork at all. They gobbled food as fast as they could. If more food was on offer, they would eat and eat until they were nearly sick. They had been used to eating at fast food restaurants during their time in foster care; it was quick and easier. Hunger was a time bomb. I could tell when they were getting hungry, because their behaviour and anxiety would escalate rapidly. They would have flashbacks to not having enough to eat when they were hungry, or being left in their pushchairs with no food at all. I did away with knives and forks. I got small plates. I put out their food and we sat and ate together. Initially it was just finger food. At 08.00 it was breakfast, at 12.00 it was lunch, at 16.30 it was tea, and at 19.00 it was supper. Access to food was restricted – otherwise they would steal food and binge, they would gobble a whole packet of biscuits. Healthy snacks were available just in case. Cola was banned. I don't think it was actually cola that made them go "hyper"; I think maybe it was that they were told it made them hyper. One time I put some cola into a drink bottle and said it was lemonade and they were fine, but I wasn't going to risk it a second time!

They were both like toddlers, living by routine: struggling when plans were inadvertently changed. Surprises were an absolute "no-go" area. They needed constant monitoring and supervision. Not until they were asleep could I stand down, but even then I had to be on alert. There were many "incidents"; some are now funny to look back on. The time James decided to bake a cake. Ingredients: three eggs – including the shells, some flour and a lot of margarine, a lot of sugar, and then some more sugar. Mix for a short time. Put bowl and metal spoon into microwave for 26 minutes… I heard the microwave "ping" on and on…

One birthday I got them balloons with flashing lights inside. They were really good, changing colour as they moved. James decided to investigate the lights inside the balloon. For some reason he swallowed the light including the battery. We spent the next couple of days inspecting the toilet for a flashing light. It took two days.

We never got those particular balloons again...

Another time Tom decided to change the light bulb in his bedside lamp. He then put his finger into the empty bulb socket. He screamed from the shock – both electric and surprise. There was a slight burn on his finger. He has not done it since, so at least it was a lesson learnt. Surprisingly, we never had any emergency trips to the local accident and emergency unit.

Our first Christmas

Tom and James had moved in nine months previously. I was still on adoption leave, so had time to prepare. I wanted to make new memories. To create new traditions. To create some magic.

The house resembled a garden centre with a festive display. There were lights everywhere. Tinsel hung off absolutely everything. We baked. We made a gingerbread house, which collapsed. We delivered cards. We went to the big church for the carol service.

Christmas Eve came. We watched Father Christmas' progress on the internet. We put out reindeer food on the lawn. We changed into new Christmas pyjamas. We put out a little bottle of beer and a mince pie for Santa. They went to bed surprisingly easily. Not a sound. I sprinkled flour on the floor in front of the fireplace and put boot prints leading to each of the sacks of presents. All was calm. All was peaceful.

As dawn began to break I could hear their REALLY loud whispers, 'Could we?' 'Should we?' 'Let's ask!' A herd of elephants descended into my room. We went downstairs, we flung the door open. Gasps of 'He's been, he's actually been!' Followed by...'Why has he put flour everywhere? I can't open anything until I've cleared up.' Out came the vacuum cleaner. 07.37 on our first Christmas morning together, and James was cleaning!

I had purposely only put a selection of presents out, so as not to overwhelm them. We undid wrappings. We tried things out and on. We found the batteries, and then we found some more batteries that worked.

We had breakfast, with the intention of opening more presents after breakfast. I asked if they had got what they wanted for Christmas. Tom looked at me and said, 'Yes, a family Christmas.'

I learnt a great deal that first Christmas. It now has to be precisely planned. No surprises and the same traditions. If one tradition is missed there is an inquest that can last for days. Tom hates the lead-up to Christmas, he hates the decorations, he hates the shopping; he likes the social side, but hates the preparation. The lack of routine can send him into a panic. James conversely loves it all, wrapped up, in a gift bag, tied with ribbon and bow. The house lights can be seen from the International Space Station. Both boys are individuals; they have experienced similar things but have been affected in different ways.

We used to go to the local dog rescue centre as volunteer dog walkers. We have always wanted a dog, but would not have the time to commit to one properly. So walking the dogs on a Saturday morning proved a good second best. It also allowed discussions around why the dogs were there. On one occasion Tom read out one of the dog's profiles.

Kane is very confused. He was happy living with his owner for many years, he felt loved. Then his owner found someone else to love and had no time for him, and sent him away.

James asked, 'How will he trust anyone again?'

Tom replied, 'Everyone can trust and love again...'

Secondary years

All that was eight years ago. The last eight years feel as though we have gone from crisis to another fallout to the next drama. I have coped with more than I ever thought was possible. But we are together. We are stronger. We are a team. I always wished I had written a diary to remember the stories, the happy and the sad, but whirlwinds don't allow you time to think, hurricanes make you live from one moment to the next. I did, though, start writing a blog online.

Things have calmed over the years. There was no quick fix, and they certainly are not fixed. The screaming and rampaging have settled. Now aged 15, the boys get on much better than most siblings, possibly due to their totally different personalities, their shared journey, or their twin bond. Who knows? The trauma, though, never, ever leaves them; we are still learning to live with that. Its manifestations have evolved and changed as their understanding of their past has matured. They no longer believe they lived an idyllic life, and that they were snatched away by the bogey man and nasty social workers, but they still cannot comprehend how they had to battle daily for survival when they were small. How they witnessed unspeakable events. How the shadows at night still haunt them. The initial chaos has left me with two confused, scared and sometimes extremely angry individuals.

Sleeping

Bedtimes are still an issue – they need to go to bed earlier than their peers. Bedtime still has to be structured around a strict routine. Holidays really upset the apple cart. Unlike their peers, they don't have televisions in their rooms. Electronic devices would keep them awake and are disconnected, and there would always be the risk of exposing them to something that might trigger their emotions. Tom goes to bed with his music on. He doesn't like loud noise, but he finds the silence deafening. In the silence, he can hear the house noises, and that scares him. We live in a relatively new house, and it still creaks, the heating groans, and these sounds take him back to his primitive time, when noise meant chaos, raised voices and mean words. Silence meant terror, sheer terror. So he listens to CDs, usually the same one, night in night out. It keeps him feeling safe. I go in, every night, to check on him, and turn his music off when he is asleep.

Conversely, James hates to have a light on. It has to be pitch black. If not, he can see shadows, silhouettes dancing across his walls. Cars driving past would shine their lights onto his ceiling and down the wall, casting shadows. The shadows would creep towards him, dragging him to times in the depth of his subconscious. He would see ghosts and then his imagination would run wild. The blackout blinds became essential.

Both of the boys have their beds against the wall. They can see the windows, they can see the door, only the wall is behind them. For many years bedtimes were fraught with anger, fear or even terror. Bad things happened at night time in their birth family: there was a lot of violence and shouting. I used to dread the bedtime routine, but over the years, with the constant repetition, the nurturing, the reassurance, bedtime now means sleep. When we were all tired, exhausted most of the time, it didn't help their mood or their behaviour. Sleep now, most of the time, feels like a safe haven. But a chink in the routine can still be a recipe for chaos.

Support?

When the boys arrived, life became a catalogue. A catalogue of meetings – with school, with social workers, psychologists. A catalogue of courses. If there was a course, I did it. I was desperate for answers, for tips, for strategies on how to cope and keep them contained. My certificates for the courses were catalogued. Parenting classes – because I was a single adopter. Attachment courses. Trauma courses. I started to talk like a therapist. 'I can hear what you are saying by the way you are shouting at me' and 'Oh gee, look how well you have done!!!'

I catalogued all the professionals who came and went, and then a new one was brought in, asking to hear the same story, saying how well we had done. We went to a social services event once, when the twins were about eight and they had been with me a year. A social worker came up to me and asked who I was, and who I had brought. She said she couldn't believe we were still together after so long; she had heard about us, she said, but it was never believed we would cope. I think that was the point when I thought: everyone else has let Tom and James down, I will not.

We have had seven or eight social workers (lost count), I have met four educational psychologists, nine adoption support workers (through social services or charities), one psychiatrist, two paediatricians, and four CAMHS workers. I have also spoken to one journalist and one radio interviewer. All wanting to hear our story, praising our efforts, then all leaving and moving on. If I felt abandoned by some professionals, how must the boys have felt? Each time a professional left, it reinforced their feeling that adults can't be trusted and would eventually leave them. At first I was really eager to share our problems and seek out help, but as time went by, and I realised that they come and go, I became despondent.

The one person we did find, by total luck, was a child psychologist. She was trained to work with traumatised children. She understood the importance of attachment, and attachment disorder. She taught us about PACE (playfulness, acceptance, curiosity and empathy). She "got us" – she understood the boys and me. She stuck around. She listened, she supported, and she helped us explore our issues. I still think the work she did with us kept us together. Our sessions went on for nearly two years. Each session was with one boy at a time, and always with me. I would have a few minutes to debrief alone, and then Tom or James would join us. Some of the sessions were filmed; we got the DVDs recently. Watching them now shows how far we have come. How much the boys have grown but also matured. This therapy was perfect for us. It was hard work, and intense at times, but it helped.

What about me?

Secondary trauma is something well documented in families where trauma that has been experienced by individuals then affects others. I have had the physical signs. I have had palpitations when I feel something is about to happen; it can simply be a look in one of the boys' eyes. My heart will start pounding; a feeling of panic fills me. I have a feeling of dread that something awful is going to happen, without knowing how it will end. I try to keep calm, I find myself something to do, but I have to stay with them. I start a random conversation – a positive one, a funny story, something to distract, anything. I offer food, a drink. I know that hunger is a trigger for them, so offering nourishment can re-attune them to know that they are safe. We still sometimes play hide and seek. At their age, and with their size, hiding places are at a premium, but it helps them to remember that they are safe and will be found. We play it like we did years ago – I pretend to be unable to find them and then, of course, I do.

On a night, I often sit in utter silence after the boys have gone to bed, so I can listen to check if they are going into each other's room to wind each other up. Invariably it is after midnight when I manage to get to bed myself. I often wait for them to settle before I start to sort myself out. I will then send off emails to school, to let them know of the latest saga, so that the teachers can watch out, and at least they have heard my side of the story. If the boys are up late, they will be tired and that will have a knock-on effect at school.

I do have a fantastic group of friends. Like everyone, I pick and choose to whom I tell what, but I do have some friends to whom I tell a lot. Most of the time there is nothing they can do, but just listen and be there, and most of the time that is enough. My parents are extremely supportive. They do what they can: my mother is sometimes the bedrock of my sanity. My father finds the boys' behaviour bizarre to challenging, but he is able to be practical and supports in his own way.

Flashbacks and meltdowns

Last year a colleague at work told me that they had thought of me the day before. She asked if we had had any meltdowns recently. Why did she ask, I wanted to know. She explained that their son had had a meltdown, and told me what a meltdown was to her: a stroppy outburst; a defiance to an instruction; a refusal to eat tea. She then said that our "meltdowns" sounded horrific, long lasting and unrelenting.

It is very rare that Tom and James have a meltdown at the same time, but when they do, it is spectacular. A meltdown is usually triggered by something, a sight – a police car driving past; a sound – the fire alarm going off at school; a smell – it used to be cigarette smoke. Tiredness is never good; the boys cannot contain their emotions as well as their tiredness. These triggers can snatch them from the here and now and plunge them back into their past. They can lose control of everything: their emotions, their senses – the only safe feeling for

SECTION II

them then is anger. They cannot hear me, or register what I am saying.

Years ago, the twins once went for absolute meltdown together. It went on for hours. I tried everything. Eventually, just before midnight, I calmly walk past the debris – furniture strewn around rooms, toys everywhere, bedding thrown down the stairs. I walk through the screaming and shouting; I go to the downstairs toilet, to where the fuse box is, and flick the switch. I plunge the house into darkness. I keep telling them that they are safe, but that I am in charge; I am not going to hurt them; I am not going to let anyone else hurt them, but I say that all this has to stop. The lights will not go on until they are quiet. They stop screaming. I put the lights on. They stop panicking. We tidy up. We all go to bed. (That is the fuse box story in a nutshell!)

In the heat of the moment, during a rant, or simply because they want to, they will hurl verbal abuse at me. Some of their words are unbelievably hurtful. Most of the time I manage to hide how disgusted I am by their verbal diarrhoea. It is coming from a place in the past. It is their primitive brain working in overdrive, their "toddler speak". I know this, but sometimes it simply cuts deep, or adds vinegar to the wounds. Some of the words I have been called – and I apologise if they offend – have been: disabled, ugly, idiot, freak, blind, deaf, stupid, awful, hated, unloved, unpopular, spotty, lonely, and worse than their parents…those are the ones I can spell and remember off the top of my head! Of course they also have a whole dictionary of swear words – some I do not even know the meaning of.

I use a range of different responses: 'Can you spell that?',

Score out of ten: 'Severrrn!', 'Technically, I am not deaf;
I wear a hearing aid, so really I am hard of hearing';
'I wonder if we could get a disabled parking badge?';
'You really are thinking this one through?'; 'Yeah, you're
probably right, I am feeling very unloved at the moment';
'Oh my god, it's a miracle! I was disabled, but now I
can walk!'; 'Do I smell? Oh, thanks, I'll put some more
deodorant on – want to borrow some?' I am careful not
to be sarcastic, derogatory or patronising. Often I simply
ignore. Certain words I address later, to ensure that they
know what they mean, or I ask if they would say those
words to people we know, who have disabilities. I make
up a story to help them reflect. 'I wonder how Grandma
would feel if someone called her deaf?' We have also had
a swear box that would have paid off Greece's national
debt. Sometimes, though, the words still hurt.

The last real meltdown with them both was last year.
They were happening less often, but when they did,
it was scary and lonely. (Years ago, when a meltdown
happened I called the police. The young rookie
policeman arrived and proceeded to give me a lecture
on parenting.) The last episode involved a lot of
aggression, aimed at me, and intimidating behaviour. They
were both taller and stronger than me by then, and they
knew it. Both went into flashback mode: re-living their
traumatic experiences, re-enacting their past. They had
blank expressions. I couldn't reason with them. I couldn't
talk logically. I simply had to hold on. I had to face the
storm. That is when it becomes scary and lonely.

This meltdown didn't last too long, just four hours or so.
I had to block a couple of fists aimed at my face. I got the
absolute anger, the look of hatred, the barrage of utter
nastiness. I had learnt a valuable lesson a couple of years

SECTION II

73

earlier; I had learnt that I had to show that I was not
afraid of them, that I would not flinch. They need me to
be invincible, to be in control, and certainly not scared. If I
am scared, bad things could happen, really bad things.

It was just after midnight on New Year's Eve, when the
twins were nearly 14. We were simply sitting at home,
watching Big Ben and the fireworks on television. Then
it was bedtime and all hell broke out. In a blink, Tom was
in my face. Screaming at me. He says everyone hates me.
He tells me I have no friends, no one finds me funny.
I can smell his breath. He tilts his head, slightly, as he
spews more vile words at me. He is constantly staring
at me. He doesn't blink. His pupils are fixed on me. His
eyes are begging me to retaliate. He needs me to hit
him, to fight back, to show him how bad he is. I must not
flinch. I must not blink. I keep within his line of vision
while he is pointing his finger in my face and screaming.
He screams in my face how disgusting my breath is. I tell
him he needs to move back so he cannot smell it, but I
cannot step back. No matter how much he swears, no
matter how angry he gets, no matter how close he gets
to me, no matter what, I cannot let him find a chink in
my armour. I have to keep constant, I have to maintain
eye contact, I dare not flinch.

I then made the conscious decision that this was
domestic abuse. I should be open and honest. I started
to tell people. I told the school – they arranged a
meeting of professionals to support us. I told my family
– they continued to be amazing. I shared our story with
friends I could trust, with friends who would not judge,
with friends who would continue to love us and respect
us. I am a member of several online groups that provide
that collective support and friendship.

Reaching out and sharing helps; it doesn't get rid of the problem, but it stops you feeling so shocked and alone. I have to remind myself of what our therapist has taught me – that the boys are testing me, to see if they will be sent away. They are sure they will be, so it is preferable to get rid of me first. It had happened before, how could they trust again?

Pushing me away – terrified to lose me

I know that the boys need me; they need to see how far they can push me away and to make sure that I will still be there. This became very apparent when I was ill and off work last year. It was nothing serious, but I did spend time moping around the house. The boys' world fell apart; they must have thought I was going to die. They never said it, but I'm sure they feared it deep inside. There were incidents every day I was off work. Tom tried to run away, he was seen racing across a field. I was hardly able to drive, but I managed to track him on the mobile phone, locate him and pick him up. He didn't really want to run away, he needed to know I would rescue him. A couple of days later, school saw an email and warned me that Tom had arranged to meet someone to buy drugs. I had to get Tom off the school bus.

James wrote a suicide note in class and made it so obvious that his teacher noticed and took it off him to see what it was. I went to school to collect him – to show that I was still there for him. I went back to work, and the urgent calls from school stopped. I sent them text messages, emails, left post-it notes in their school planners. To show I was thinking of them. To show them I was still around.

I have been lucky with work. The boys' secondary school contains things the best they can; they contact me only in extreme situations. That means I can focus fully at work, become my professional self, away from the trauma of home life. My work is to support families; I go to meetings and work alongside other professionals to advocate and get the best for children and their families. I am articulate and assertive, able to get my views across. I put my professional hat on. It took a long time for me to realise that this was what I also had to do when I was at meetings about my own children. I was often battle-worn, with rock bottom self-esteem. When I went to a meeting I would find it hard to even explain what was happening at home. Even though I knew something was right, I would not be able to convey what I thought. I had to learn that I could not be a parent and emotionally involved during these meetings; I had to detach myself and become my professional self.

Broken ties

Last year Tom broke his collarbone. It was a football injury, a total accident. It happened after a tackle during a football match at school. He heard the bone crack. I got the call everyone dreads (at least he had not done anything wrong!); I went to school to collect him. We waited in the busy Casualty to have the news that he had fractured his clavicle, he would need to wear a sling, he would need to come back to fracture clinic in a week, he would need regular painkillers. All the usual stuff.

For a day or so he was dutifully patient – wearing his sling as a symbol of his heroism. Then the pain got more manageable and the sling became an irritant. Maybe he was cured already? Maybe they were wrong? Maybe his bone could change the whole of medical science and heal itself in less than four days. He started to take his sling off. He would swing his arms around. He was falling out with people. His mood swings went from placid and loveable to hostile and aggressive. He is a teenager, so of course he is invincible, he is immortal. But when he was younger, he had been neglected. He had been left alone. He went without food. His needs were not met. His body coped because his brain wired itself to survive in the most hostile environment. When he hurt himself no one would come. Remember, once he was left in the sun as a toddler until he got burnt and was admitted to hospital. The adults didn't help or care. They didn't keep him safe. So now, years later, despite being nurtured and secure, his brain was fighting to keep him safe. How could he trust anyone? Why would anyone look after him? After all, when he was helpless, he was neglected. Now he is older, he is able to look after himself, and to defend himself.

Tom was found with a whole packet of 12 paracetamols in his pocket. I do believe they were for his pain, nothing else. He needed to take control of managing his pain, in case he was let down again. He took his sling off because he had to be better, he couldn't remain injured. In the same way the lion will go after the weakest antelope in the herd, he has to be strong or else he will himself be attacked. Tom would make a production of taking his sling off, he would be saying, 'Look, I am better!', whilst inside he would be shouting, 'I am frightened! I don't know what to do!' He turned against those nearest to him, pushing them away; he might as well, because they will reject him anyway. His rugby team, who were all his mates, will now forget him and move on. As though he were the most diligent meerkat that is soon rejected and forgotten after the smallest misdemeanour.

77

So at home we went back to basics. We have to be safe. We wonder why he won't keep his sling on. We find compromises but stick to the rules to keep safe. I was the adult, the carer; I had to take back control – when to give painkillers, not waiting until they are needed but when they are due. I made sure the sling was comfortable. I empathised and sympathised. It was the first time he had ever really hurt himself. I didn't patronise, I listened. I built the scaffolding back up – it was just for a short time. I kept saying how quick the time was going, 'The first week is nearly over already'. We looked forward to the fracture clinic to see how the bones were mending. We found ways to do things together – easier to put the affected arm in his shirt first when getting dressed. I allowed him to be as independent as possible, but consistently offered 'Let me do that for you, to help you'. I did a running commentary on progress – he could do this or that now. We found new responsibilities for him to replace the ones he was not able to fulfil for the time being. We spent time together. We played board games every night after the accident. I took him to school instead of using the school bus. One day he said, 'I like having this time together on a morning, just you and me'.

James' behaviour also became difficult during this time. Maybe he felt he would be forgotten with all the attention given to Tom? I tried to make sure James got his share by sending him a message while I was at the hospital with Tom, buying him a snack for when we got home. I had to keep showing him I was thinking about him too.

We were re-building, mending the broken ties as well as the broken bones...

Schools and education

I'm Sorry

I'm sorry my son set off the fire alarm, again, when it was raining and cold outside.

I'm sorry he disrupted yet another lesson.

I'm sorry you heard him swearing, and shouting.

I'm sorry you actually saw him thumping the wall with his fist.

I'm sorry he smokes.

I'm sorry he makes annoying random noises.

I'm sorry I am exhausted, absolutely exhausted and don't keep in touch as much as I should.

I'm sorry that my child experienced and witnessed violence, before he lived with me.

I'm sorry that before we met, his house burnt down.

I'm sorry that he moved home between 10–20 times. Who knows? Who cares?

I'm sorry that since I adopted him I haven't fixed him.

I'm sorry because he feels sorry most of the time.

I'm sorry I keep having to prove that I won't give up on him.

I'm sorry that you don't see the amazing person I see.

I'm sorry.

School for Tom and James has always been a supreme challenge. After the summer holidays, going back to primary school would fill me with dread and fear. The phone calls would start. I would be constantly checking to see if the school had phoned to tell me the latest awful thing one of them had done. Collecting them from school would always involve the walk of shame, 'Can we have a word, please?', and the looks from other parents.

Secondary school should have been even worse. It's a massive school. It's huge! There seem to be millions of students, swarming around like ants. The school has a great academic record, and an even better zero tolerance attitude to bad behaviour. We should not have lasted long at all. However, the boys are now in their last year. Only another six months and we will have made it. So how come this high school has been so positive? There are many reasons, but based on our experience, these are my top tips for other schools that want to support pupils who have experienced trauma:

- **Good communication between staff and parents** – We are a partnership. We support each other. We have mutual respect. If something happens at home, I tell the school. Not to blame the boys, but simply so the staff are aware. Tom or James, or both, may have been unsettled the night before and tired in the morning. The school staff then know to keep a check on the boys. They put in place actions to support them, they do not wait for them to fail. If they have missed breakfast, we have a stash of food at school for them. It is about looking outside the box. They know what the triggers are, so they try to stop behaviours before they escalate.

- **Consequences** – for example, sanctions – there has to be a natural consequence for an action. If they mess about at lunch break, they miss their next break. Consequences have to be timely, there and then, not in a week's time. My two simply will not remember what they have done wrong even a day later, or their story will have changed so much that they believe they are being victimised by the staff.

- **Close working together** within teams at school. Our school has a well-run student support structure; the staff members communicate with each other about the boys. They know if they are having a bad day or if they are having a great day. They know about incidents before the boys arrive at their lesson. They use all manner of communication, from radios to email. In this day and age it is so easy to keep in touch. The school now only tells me about things after the event. They see their role as complementary to mine; they look after the boys at school, I look after them at home. We are seen as a united front by the boys. At the primary school the boys knew there was conflict, and exploited it: usually by saying 'Dad said this' or 'my teacher said the other'.

- **Not blaming the parents** of traumatised children for their behaviour. The staff at the school know I am trying to do my best. They know the boys' outbursts are not my fault. No matter how bad things are at school, the staff know I have seen and experienced

81

worse at home. They ask for my advice, they listen to what I have to say, and they **hear me**. They are a fantastic support to me as well as to Tom and James. When we are having a quiet patch (it does happen sometimes), school gets in touch to check that everything is OK.

- **Supporting each other** – Staff need to support each other and to be able to debrief, which allows new starts and prevents secondary trauma affecting the teachers who are supporting my children.

- **Changing the paradigms** – Our school looks for success – changing the way to see things. They are constantly finding positives about the boys – catching them being good. They put constructive comments in their planner – so I can see what they've achieved during the day. These strategies do take time to plan and devise, but dealing with meltdowns and reactive behaviour takes much longer, and uses more staff. A simple positive word of praise can save the whole day. The teachers also "check in" with the boys. Just a 'Hello Tom' or a nod at the beginning of the lessons allows them to feel they have been noticed, that they are safe.

- **Treating each child as an individual** – Our school does not treat Tom and James the same, and treats all children as individuals. Despite my two being twins, they are not compared to each other. They are not asked why they are not like the other. The staff at the school do not try to force square pegs into round holes.

- **Learning from each other** – Learning from me,

from other staff and from other professionals. What works, what doesn't? And being aware that this can always change.

School continues to be a struggle for my two, but they love going. They feel included, they feel supported, and they feel safe. If they have had a bad day the day before, they go back knowing it's a new start. There are no repercussions; they are not reminded of past poor behaviour. They are moved forward. The teachers don't always get it right, but neither do I. Sometimes we have to blunder our way through, picking up the pieces as we go along.

We have been so lucky with the support we have had from our secondary school. I do not know how we would have survived as a family had it not been there for us. School life plays a massive part in any child's life; they are there so much of their time. Schools need to appreciate that they can give significant help and support as well as educate. Before my children could learn to learn, they had to feel safe.

Holidays

I still remember my summer holidays as a child. I am sure they were never as idyllic as I believe they were, but they were happy times. The exciting evacuation from the caravan site at 3am due to risk of flooding. The huge dead fish we found on the beach, which we saved for fishing bait, only to find the family dog eating it a few days later. Running down sand dunes so fast I nearly started to fly. Watching the salmon jumping upstream in Scotland. They were snippets of time, but they are embedded in my mind. In my adult years I have travelled and explored some exotic and fantastic places – far flung and nearby. I was more than happy to jump on a plane and travel for hours. I loved the hustle and bustle of cities. I loved exploring and finding my way around. I always planned and booked, I could never have been a backpacker and not known exactly where I was going, but I enjoyed my time away. I adore the countryside too. I love photography and taking picture after picture of scenery – one day I will go through the old photos and record where they were taken! My favourite thing is sunsets. Above water, across a landscape. Watching the scene change before my eyes. Then it's gone, recorded on the Facebook in your mind (or even on Facebook!).

Change for Tom and James means leaving, means being taken away – flashbacks to a dark time. They moved a lot, under very stressful circumstances. When they first came to me, simply packing an overnight bag produced terror. I would have to pack for them, still do sometimes.

These days holidays are short breaks, four or five days away at most. We have managed to try different places, after having been back to exactly the same place, time after time. We don't go far, in case we need to come back, in case it all proves too much. Last year we managed a last-minute bargain, a gorgeous converted barn in the country, and at half the price as it was a late deal.

Needless to say, most of the time was spent trying to be therapeutic, being understanding, showing lots of empathy, letting things go, or simply treating them like toddlers. That's OK, because that's what I do most of the time, in order to keep things contained. I am not sure if that holiday was any worse than previous ones; perhaps I was tired, and felt it was time for me to chill out? Whatever, it was hard, extremely hard work.

The first night there was screaming, shouting and slamming of doors. They needed to be in control, but they were in chaos. The second day was spent doing loads of physical things, to wear them out. A long walk followed by swimming. They slept that night! The next day fishing and a boat trip. In the evening they argued about beds – who was sleeping where. Tom was arguing for hours. He was too tired to do anything the next day, so I took James out. Later, Tom continued to be aggressive, swearing at me and threatening. He calmed for a while. I tried to say we should go home, and then James turned on me. Nothing physical, yet. James was really tired. He didn't want to have his "holiday" spoiled. I packed my bag and tidied the kitchen. There was a stand-off, the tension was palpable. I stayed calm, but kept being told to f*** off and f***ing shut up. Should I sit it out? Pack and go? Wait for things to escalate and call the police to turf us out?

Somehow I went into ultra-fantastic dad mode. I was very sympathetic to the needs of both. I was hearing and listening to both. I laid on the therapeutic understanding thickly, saying how well we work together as a team. We had their favourite tea. We had a games night. At the end of one game I said how much I had enjoyed it, and how glad I was that I had decided we didn't need to go home. We played another game – Scrabble of all things! Then I sent them to bed. They went straight to sleep! I was absolutely shattered. Really shattered. When they are away, their behaviour is toddler-like. Their overwhelming feeling is that of fear. It was an awful "holiday". We haven't been away overnight since that time. We enjoy ourselves going for days out. I make sure we explore cities, I enjoy the scenery. I let people "like" the pictures on Facebook of "another stunning sunset".

I wonder what they will remember in years to come. The boat ride? Catching the fish? Swimming in the outdoor pool? The sunsets?

Railway man

A while ago I watched *The Railway Man*. A poignant film, starring Colin Firth. It described the trauma suffered by prisoners in concentration camps during the Second World War. The flashbacks were horrific. The suffering and anguish went on long after the prisoners returned home. They tried to live normal lives, but lived with their haunting past.

The boys watched the film, without too many interruptions or too many questions, which is testament enough to the film's quality. But halfway through Tom said, 'That man really suffered, didn't he? Bad things happened to him. Is that why I do things I don't understand too?'

James responded, 'I bet more happened to them that they don't show in the film. More that was too scary to show.'

I will never fully know what happened to the boys in the past. They were too young to actually remember the events that traumatised them. What I do see are the emotional scars. I see the effects of trauma displayed and acted out. I am aware when they have flashbacks. I can also see how much they have changed. I can see that the jigsaw pieces of their lives are slowly fitting together to make a complete picture. It may not be a happy, picturesque landscape, but it allows Tom and James to have a better understanding of what has made them who they are. We blunder our way through life. I am not perfect; I know my flaws (they tell me all the time what they are!). We live each day as it comes. I try not to look too far into the future, but when I look back, you know what? Yes, we do make a good team!

Useful organisations

Listed below are a short selection of organisations which can provide information and assistance in meeting the needs of children who may have been affected by experiencing trauma.

The Anna Freud Centre

Provides services to families and children with emotional, behavioural and developmental difficulties, and also conducts research into the effectiveness of psychotherapy techniques and children's emotional development.

12 Maresfield Gardens
London NW3 5SU
Tel: 020 7794 2313
www.annafreud.org

Association for Child and Adolescent Mental Health

An association for professionals who are involved with children. It arranges seminars and publishes professional journals, but does not

provide an advice service.
St Saviour's House
39–41 Union Street
London SE1 1SD
Tel: 020 7403 7458
www.acamh.org.uk

British Association for Counselling and Psychotherapy (BACP)

Provides details of local counsellors and psychotherapists.
BACP House, 15 St John's Business Park
Lutterworth
Leicestershire LE17 4HB
Tel: 01455 883300
www.bacp.co.uk

Caspari Foundation (formerly Forum for the Educational Therapy and Therapeutic Teaching, FAETT)

Promotes educational therapy and therapeutic learning to help children
who have emotional barriers that can impair learning. Provides courses
for teachers as well as consultations for children and parents.
Finspace
225–229 Seven Sisters Road
London N4 2DA
Tel: 020 7527 5161
www.caspari.org.uk

The Centre for Child Mental Health

Aims to increase awareness of emotional well-being and mental health
of children. It conducts research, provides information for parents,
teachers and professionals, and provides seminars on child mental
health topics.
2–18 Britannia Row
London N1 8PA

Tel: 020 7354 2913

www.childmentalhealthcentre.org

Family Futures

An adoption and adoption support agency which specialises in therapeutic work for children who have experienced early trauma and who have attachment difficulties.

3 & 4 Floral Place

7–9 Northampton Grove

London N1 2PL

Tel: 020 7354 4161

www.familyfutures.co.uk